Other Side of the Coin

Alex Ndukwe

Copyright © 2019 Alex Ndukwe

All rights reserved

This book or any portion thereof may not be reproduced or used without the express written permission of the publisher except for the use of brief quotations in a book review

First printing, 2019

Printed in the united states of America

ISBN: 978-0-359-81405-3

Dedication

To families that have lost their relatives and loved ones to suicide due to economic challenges and hardship.

Table of Contents

Dedication

Forward

Introduction

Chapter 1: Issues we must Understand

Applying Faith

   Examination

Chapter 2: The Man Called Job

God's Perception

The tempter

Series of Attacks ....

Chapter 3: Are you in a storm now?

Foreword

Brethren Christianity is not a bed of rosses and I believe most matured children of God are fully aware of this. We must experience trials or tribulation, the enemy might even tempt us.

But in all these we are more than conquerors (Romans 8:37) , I want to encourage those passing through challenges at this point in time , all will be well in the name of Jesus.

Depression is not the answer but prayer and studying the word of God is bound to make us stronger and make us understand God the more.

This book is aimed at encouraging and the same time explain in details reasons why examination is a must for children of God and I pray the Lord will see us through.

Introduction

The other side of the coin, things has fallen apart and it's a different ball game now, we intend to review the travails of the great man called job, from my discoveries no one as ever suffered like this man and he continued to be steadfast and remained on the part of righteousness and most importantly never derailed, never fell out of track.

What are you passing through now, are you aware that all hope is not lost, the Lord Jesus is able to deliver you, suicide is not an option, we are not unaware of the hardship every citizen of Nigeria is passing through. You might not have a stable income or you are heavily in debts, you lost your job , that's not enough for you to jump into the Lagoon , drink snipper , strangle yourself , hope is available at the feet of JESUS if only you can belief.

In this season there are lot's of lesson that we must learn, the one that has lost his job in a very lucrative sector like Banking, Telecom, oil & gas etc. , should understand that it's an opportunity to become an employer of Labour , add your quota to nation building.

You could be an investor and lost your resources , there is need to review the root cause of such loses and trust God for wisdom to recover from such challenges , this might also mean that you are owing business associates a lot of debts and difficulties in managing the situation as pressure is mounted and there's no way out , it calls for a deep reflection and trust God for a way out.

Suicide is not the way out, when this happens you commit a sin, you cannot terminate a life God created , no matter the situation , this action takes the individual to the pit of hell , the problem is not solved, the culprit only leaves the scene.

I refer you to my book on 'what's in your heart?' , our actions reveals that the heart of the culprit is far from God , such a fellow is vulnerable and becomes easily influenced by the enemy and before you know it, mayhem is unleashed and his/her relatives would be in pains. No man on earth has suffered like Job, this led to the review of this man's life and we need to pick some lessons from it.

Unfortunately our society only respect the wealthy rather than intellects, even in the church of God, Pastors prefer to reserve roles for the most successful in the congregation, believing that it's the only way they can spend for God, quality workers/ministers that are struggling with their finances and have intellectual expertise cannot play any role, this is rather unfortunate and I'm speaking from experience.

Though this is not our focus but it should be mentioned, it triggers pressure on our brethren, I recall the story of the minister that stole 35 million Naira in his place of work because he wants to sow in a church building projects , what kind of seed is this , corruptible but men of God will gladly collect and thank God for it , but they will not inquire from God whether to accept such donations or not , the Lord will help our pastors in Jesus name.

As a pastor when last did you seek the face of the Lord before accepting an offering or a gift from a member of your congregation or anyone that wants to sow in your life, it's no longer a practice today.

This season calls for us to re-strategize and success will be within our reach, need to eliminate waste of resources during plenty, during famine survival will not be far from us and this is a valid fact. We need to understand that economies around the world are struggling, the season calls for creativity, effective management and deployment of resources.

As Christians we need to dispel fears of the unknown, 2 timothy 1:7 says 'For God hath not given us the spirit of fear, but power, and love, and of a sound mind'

Chapter 1

Issues We Must Understand

As children of God we need to understand some things, the enemy is engaging in soul winning and when we make attempts to depopulate their kingdom he is not happy but will unleash attack. We must be prepared and continue in our quest of soul winning.

There is no compromise, holiness is key in our Christian race. We need to work out our salvation with fear and trembling. These days the kind of messages we hear is disgusting, for example, 'one saved, forever saved', meaning you can commit sin as a child of God and you can still make it to heaven, grace covers you. What an error. That is a direct flight to hell.

The enemy is very ticklish, his agents have entered the church of God and have even become pastors. May the Lord help his church in the name of Jesus. Heresies are been preached and makes it easy to lure as many as possible to hell.

Tribulation, temptation for a child of God is a must. Christianity is not a bed of roses, storms must come, may you remain victorious in Jesus name. Let us discuss Applying Faith & Examination.

Applying Faith

'Now faith is the substance of things hoped for, the evidence of things not seen' (Heb 11:1.)

Faith is the pivot of Christianity. It can launch you beyond one's expectation, but we should be applied practically, and we should not underestimate what the almighty God can do for those that exhibit this trait, it should not be abused.

Faith should be applied when we desire a miracle, even when desired result has not been attained, push again with more measure of it, don't give up, results must be attained. I have this testimony, my Honda accord vehicle could not select gear correctly, I called my mechanic and after his candid examination, he recommended that the gear box be replaced.

I picked up an handkerchief blessed by General overseer of Redeemed Christian Church of God during the convection, I layed it on the gear of the car and made a declaration , 'Faulty gear receive life in the name of Jesus', I believed it was settled, 30 minutes later, I decided to drive the car once more and discovered that there was a tremendous improvement, the box selected effectively and I was astonished.

I sent for the mechanic and asked him to test the car and he confirmed that it was working correctly and he enquired from me to know how I resolved it and simply told him that the Ancient of Days helped me to resolve the problem. I drove this car for another 3 years, till the day I sold it. Be it spiritual or physical problem, faith was put into action and it delivered the solution, Halleluyah!

In the quest of applying faith, some preachers tend to deceive members of their congregations during counselling or when there are challenges. Our religious Leaders should come alive with their responsibilities by ensuring that they meet the needs of their followers physically and spiritually for example, if someone brings up a challenge ,'He/She has not had food for a week now' , the problem at hand must be resolved immediately before counselling.

We appreciate God for different flavours of ministries all over the world, we have holiness, prosperity, signs & wonders pastors, there is an important phenomenon we have to deal with, Most times our sermons fail to tell members of the congregation some basic truths about our Christian race, often it is very positive because burdens must be lifted, encouraging ourselves is very important but must be embedded with the truth and make us understand that storms will definitely come , we must not give up but look beyond the situation and allow the burden bearer to take charge(Mathew 11:28)

Trials can lead into atheism. When your faith is small the devil can rip it out. Don't let him put you in despair and bitterness towards God. Don't ever forget the other times God has delivered you because He will do it again. The devil will try to say it was a coincidence, but with God there is no coincidence. Cry out to God. Block Satan off and always remember that we have victory in Christ.

Most of us are in the habit of having an option 'B' for any challenge that comes our way while exercising faith and most times we embrace it and this negates the essence of waiting upon the Lord for the appointed time.

I remember when I said, "why God, why this, and why that?" God told me to wait for His timing. God has delivered me in the past, but when you are going through bad times all you're thinking about is right now. I've seen God use trials to build me up, answer different prayers, open doors, help others, and I've seen many miracles where I knew it was only God who could have done this. (Fritz Chery)

Applying faith, we should know when an individual's heart is divided. It becomes extremely difficult for such a fellow to exercise faith, already he/she has lost hope and doesn't see how things will ever improve, we need to help such a person so that he/she can recover and exercise faith like a mustard seed.

I'm particularly impressed to see some pastors that are successful professionals counsel their members with all the knowledge that they possess and not leaving out the spiritual aspect, all hands must be on deck to support those in crises, we might be saving a life from suicide.

Examination

This is basically trial or tribulation and the Lord cannot tempt his children, Jerimiah 29:11, 'For I know the thoughts that I think toward you, saith the LORD, thoughts of peace, and not of evil, to give you an expected end.' Most of us make statements like 'God why tempt me' , delete this from you dictionary, the enemy tempts because he want to destroy and win the victim into his kingdom. God allows examinations because of the following reasons:

1) Trials help our perseverance.

   It make us to persevere and wait upon the Lord, remain unshakable and at the end victory is assured, James 1:12 "God blesses those who patiently endure testing and temptation. Afterward they will receive the crown of life that God has promised to those who love him."

2) Sometimes we suffer because of our own mistakes. Another thing is we should never test God.

   In my life I've suffered because I followed the wrong voice. I did my will instead of God's will. I can't blame God for my mistakes, but what I can say is God brought me through it and made me stronger and smarter in the process, Hosea 4:6 "My people are destroyed from lack of knowledge. "Because you have rejected knowledge, I also reject you as my priests; because you have ignored the law of your God, I also will ignore your children."

3) **God is making you humble.**

The situation at hand would make us humble and mould us the way the Lord want us to be. 2 Corinthians 12:7 "even though I have received such wonderful revelations from God. So to keep me from becoming proud, I was given a thorn in my flesh, a messenger from Satan to torment me and keep me from becoming proud."

4) **God's discipline.**

Hebrews 12:5-11 "And have you completely forgotten this word of encouragement that addresses you as a father addresses his son? It says, "My son, do not make light of the Lord's discipline, and do not lose heart when he rebukes you, because the Lord disciplines the one he loves, and he chastens everyone he accepts as his son." Endure hardship as discipline; God is treating you as his children. For what children are not disciplined by their father? If you are not disciplined—and everyone undergoes discipline—then you are not legitimate, not true sons and daughters at all. Moreover, we have all had human fathers who disciplined us and we respected them for it. How much more should we submit to the Father of spirits and live! They disciplined us for a little while as they thought best; but God disciplines us for our good, in order that we may share in his holiness. No discipline seems pleasant at the time, but painful. Later on, however, it produces a harvest of righteousness and peace for those who have been trained by it."

5) **So you can become more dependent on the Lord.**

2 Corinthians 12:9-10 Each time he said, "My grace is all you need. My power works best in weakness." So now I am glad to boast about my

weaknesses, so that the power of Christ can

work through me. That's why I take pleasure in my weaknesses, and in the insults, hardships, persecutions, and troubles that I suffer for Christ. For when I am weak, then I am strong."

6) God wants to spend time with you

Revelation 2:2-5 "I know what you do, how you work hard and never give up. I know you do not put up with the false teachings of evil people. You have tested those who say they are apostles but really are not, and you found they are liars. You have patience and have suffered troubles for my name and have not given up. But I have this against you: You have left the love you had in the beginning. So remember where you were before you fell. Change your hearts and do what you did at first. If you do not change, I will come to you and will take away your lampstand from its place."

7) God could be protecting you from a bigger problem

God might just be protecting you from a bigger problem in the future , the challenge restrains a step that can lead to dangers of even death. Psalm 121:5-8 "The Lord guards you. The Lord is the shade that protects you from the sun. The sun cannot hurt you during the day, and the moon cannot hurt you at night. The Lord will protect you from all dangers; he will guard your life. The Lord will guard you as you come and go, both now and forever."

Psalm 9:7-10 "But the Lord rules forever. He sits on his throne to judge, and he will judge the world in fairness; he will decide what is fair for the nations. The Lord defends those who suffer; he defends them in times of trouble. Those who know the Lord trust him, because he will not leave those who come to him."

8) Trials help to build our faith in the Lord.

James 1:2-6 "Consider it pure joy, my

brothers and sisters, whenever you face trials of many kinds. because you know that the testing of your faith produces perseverance. Let perseverance finish its work so that you may be mature and complete, not lacking anything. If any of you lacks wisdom, you should ask God, who gives generously to all without finding fault, and it will be given to you."

9) <u>You can help someone because you have been in that situation</u>

2 Corinthians 1:3-4 "Blessed be the God and Father of our Lord Jesus Christ, the Father of mercies and God of all comfort; who comforteth us in all our affliction, that we may be able to comfort them that are in any affliction, through the comfort wherewith we ourselves are comforted of God."

Galatians 6:2 "Carry each other's burdens, and in this way you will fulfill the law of Christ."

10) To remind us that it is God who is always in control.

Luke 8:22-25 "One day Jesus said to his disciples, "Let us go over to the other side of the lake." So they got into a boat and set out. As they sailed, he fell asleep. A squall came down on the lake, so that the boat was being swamped, and they were in great danger. The disciples went and woke him, saying, "Master, Master, we're going to drown!" He got up and rebuked the wind and the raging waters; the storm subsided, and all was calm. "Where is your faith?" he asked his disciples. In fear and amazement they asked one another, "Who is this? He commands even the winds and the water, and they obey him."

11) Trials increase our knowledge and they help us learn God's Word.

Psalm 119:71-77 "It was good for me to be

afflicted so that I might learn your decrees. he law from your mouth is more precious to me than thousands of pieces of silver and gold. Your hands made me and formed me; give me understanding to learn your commands. May those who fear you rejoice when they see me, for I have put my hope in your word. I know, Lord, that your laws are righteous, and that in faithfulness you have afflicted me. May your unfailing love be my comfort, according to your promise to your servant. Let your compassion come to me that I may live, for your law is my delight."

Joseph is an example in the Bible, Gen 39:4

"And Joseph found grace in his sight, and he served him: and he made him overseer over his house, and all that he had he put into his hand."

Potiphar put joseph in charge of everything in house household because he was faithful, he didn't abuse this privilege because he had the fear of God. The first temptation was madam of the house in Gen 39:7

"And it came to pass after these things, that his master's wife cast her eyes upon Joseph; and she said, Lie with me."

This is an examination to proof if really Joseph had the fear of God and he did not allow flesh to override his senses, he could have said 'after all I'm the general overseer of Potiphar's house and I should be in charge of his wife, why can't I sleep with her'.

The young man refused this request even though this harassment continued for several days and out of frustration she implicated Joseph and the master threw him into prison, let us put ourselves in Joseph's shoes, how will you feel?

The seed of holiness triggered a mark of favour in Joseph's life, while in prison he prospered and the Lord was with him, Gen 39: 22

"And the keeper of the prison committed to Joseph's hand all the prisoners that were in the prison; and whatsoever they did there, he was the doer of it."

We know the remaining part of the story; he passed all his examinations and the lord promoted him by using Pharaoh <u>and</u> Hence, Joseph became a prime minister in the land of Egypt.

As a child of God, the lord might want to test your level of faith by setting an examination for you and if it happens that you triumph, promotion comes. We need to be dead to sin and ensure our flesh does not lure us out of the path of righteousness. We need to cleave unto the word of God, this will help us.

The Lord cannot give you an exam more than your capacity or capabilities. Examination is a continuous process in the vineyard and the lord will help all of us in the name of Jesus. What of when you fail the examination, there are categories as mentioned earlier on, depending on the calibre of student, there are some expectations, when it falls short, the punishment will be severe. An example is Moses, the lord used him to facilitate the liberation of the children of Israel from slavery that had lasted for 430 years, he had always begged God whenever the children of Israel misbehaved during their travails in the wilderness.

The instruction given to Moses was is in the book of numbers 20:8, 'Take the rod, and gather thou the assembly together, thou, and Aaron thy brother, and speak ye unto the rock before their eyes; and it shall give forth his water, and thou shalt bring forth to them water out of the rock: so thou shalt give the congregation and their beasts drink.'

Though we might say it's only an instruction , technically it's an examination, will he carry out the task to the letter so that my name will be glorified and Moses did a different thing , lets look at numbers 20:10-11, 'And Moses and Aaron gathered the congregation together before the rock, and he said unto them, hear now, ye rebels; must we fetch you water out of this rock?

And Moses lifted his hand, and with his rod he smote the rock twice: and the water came out abundantly, and the congregation drank, and their beasts also.'

The instruction was 'speak to the rock' and he smote the rock with his rod , this implies he was disobedient and he received an instant judgement from the lord , he will not enter the promise land, Numbers 20:12

'And the LORD spake unto Moses and Aaron, because ye believed me not, to sanctify me in the eyes of the children of Israel, therefore ye shall not bring this congregation into the land which I have given them.'

This man begged for the children of Israel and now there's no one to beg the lord on his behalf and he had to take the punishment because he should have followed the instruction to the letter. What of the three Hebrew boys, their examination was not an easy one because they defiled the consequences which is death and they stood their ground, they had the word of God in their system , Exodus 34:14,

'For thou shalt worship no other god: for the LORD, whose name is Jealous, is a jealous God:'

They remained unshakable, unmovable and unperturbed, even when news reached the king that they refused to bow down to the graven image, Dan 3:14 , 'Nebuchadnezzar spake and said unto them, Is it true, O Shadrach, Meshach, and Abednego, do not ye serve my gods, nor worship the golden image which I have set up?' And these boys replied the king, Dan 3:16-17 ,'Shadrach, Meshach, and Abednego answered and said to the king, O Nebuchadnezzar, we are not careful to answer thee in this matter. If it be so, our God whom we serve is able to deliver us from the burning fiery furnace, and he will deliver us out of thine hand, O king.'

The king was annoyed and he instructed that they should be cast into the furnace , this was an exam set by man and the lord helped them in this challenge , by providing the fourth person in the furnace that insulated these boys and they came out unhurt and after this incidence , they were promoted ,Dan 30:30 , 'Then the king promoted Shadrach, Meshach, and Abednego, in the province of Babylon.'

We will have to be examined before promotion will come and if we fail we cannot experience any lifting, I pray God will elevate us and we will not be missing in his kingdom.

Chapter 2
The Man called JOB

JOB resided in the of uz, was a perfect man, upright and feared God, eschewed evil. He was the greatest man in the east , blessed with 7 Sons and 3 daughters, the following assets that he had are as follows; 7,000 Sheep , 3,000 Camels , 5,000 yoke of Oxen , 5,000 She Asses.

The Lord loved him , the tempter satan approached God and the Lord asked him where are you coming from?, he answered , 'to and fro in the earth, walking up and down in it.

God asked him have you considered my servant Job, there is none like him , upright, perfect , feared the Lord.

The tempter told God that if he should touch all that he had , he will curse you at your face, the enemy confirmed if the lord had put an hedge over him and his belongings. The Lord allowed it to prove a point to the tempter, JOB 1:12 , satan struck, Job received the first bad news from one of his servants, 'Sabeans attacked and took the oxen and donkey away from the farm, all the servants were killed, he managed to escape.

Another bad news , fire from the sky, burnt up all the sheep and consumed them, what a loss. While he was pondering on what is happening to him, another news came from the another servant, the chaldeans had attacked and taken away all the camels.

The building where his children were collapsed and they all died. He didn't curse God, rather he tore his clothes, shaved his hair , the pain of all that he lost was severe and remained steadfast with the Lord.

The first assault from the enemy , the man after God's heart remained unmovable, the tempter told God that he was going to touch him skin for skin and bone for bone, he will renounce you in the face. The lord told satan that my servant is in your hands please spare his life. Satan inflicted Job with sore from the sole of his foot to his head.

Job's wife reacted and told her husband, you are still standing with the Lord, curse the Lord and die, he reprimanded her and told her why are you senseless.

The news reached his associates, Eliphaz, Bildad, Zophar, they decided to visit him and sympathize with him, when they saw their friend they could not recognize him, they started to weep, it was glaring that their friend has passed through a very difficult and heart breaking challenges.

Despite these challenges , Job cursed the day he was born, wondered why did her mother give birth to him. He made such comments, hated himself and the friend Elipaz reacted in Job 4:2, 'If someone ventures to talk with you, will you be grieved, who can withhold himself from speaking?'

He reminded Job of how he had impacted on life's positively, supported the weak with words of encouragement, but now it's your turn, the word of encouragement were reeled out by his friends, Job 4:6 - 8, Is not this thy fear, thy confidence, thy hope, and the uprightness of thy ways? 'Remember, I pray thee, whoever perished, being innocent? or where were the righteous cut off? 'Even as I have seen, they that plow iniquity, and sow wickedness, reap the same. By the blast of God, they perish, and by the breath of his nostrils are they consumed.'

His friends knew him as one that feared the Lord and he's very faithful and full of good works and such calamities should not in any way befall him. These statements were to encourage him that God will deliver him. They encouraged him with these words found in Job 5: 15-22 , 'But he saveth the poor from the sword, from their mouth, and from the hand of the mighty. So the poor hath hope, and iniquity stoppeth her mouth. Behold, happy is the man whom God correcteth: therefore despise not thou the chastening of the Almighty: For he maketh sore, and bindeth up: he woundeth, and his hands make whole.

He shall deliver thee in six troubles: yea, in seven there shall no evil touch thee. In famine he shall redeem thee from death: and in war from the power of the sword. Thou shalt be hid from the scourge of the tongue: neither shalt thou be afraid of destruction when it cometh. At destruction and famine thou shalt laugh: neither shalt thou be afraid of the beasts of the earth.'

And JOB responded in chapter 6, and his friends continued to talk to him throughout their deliberations Job never accused God but he only spoke without knowledge and carelessly , his friends could not answer him in a way that will encourage him , the engagement continued without any progress.

Job doesn't know that the Lord only allowed the enemy to set this exam and you could recall God telling the enemy before the second assault that he should not take his life.

Elihu the son of barachel got involved when he saw that these three men could not convince him and answer questions , the young man handled Job by answering him questions and accused Job of multiplying his words and not speaking with knowledge; he reiterated the greatness of God, Job 32:4-5 , and encouraged Job to stand still and consider the wondrous works of God.

The Lord answered Job out of the whirlwind and said, Job 38:2-3, 'Who is this that darkeneth counsel by words without knowledge? Gird up now thy loins like a man; for I will demand of thee and answer thou me.'

In verse 4, 'Where wast thou when I laid the foundations of the earth? declare, if thou hast understanding.' The lord made him understand that he's a great God and interestingly God reprimanded his three friends and instructed them to herefore take unto you now seven bullocks and seven rams, and go to my servant Job, and offer up for yourselves a burnt offering; and my servant Job shall pray for you: for him will I accept: lest I deal with you after your folly, in that ye have not spoken of me the thing which is right, like my servant Job.

They carried out the instruction accordingly and the Lord visited Job and he restored all he had lost in two folds.

Then came there unto him all his brethren, and all his sisters, and all they that had been of his acquaintance before, and did eat bread with him in his house: and they bemoaned him, and comforted him over all the evil that the LORD had brought upon him: every man also gave him a piece of money, and everyone an earring of gold. He had seven sons and three daughters, and the LORD blessed the latter end of Job more than his beginning: for he had fourteen thousand sheep, and six thousand camels, and a thousand yoke of oxen, and a thousand she asses.

Though he was heartbroken and cursed the day he was born and never said anything against God, he passed the exam and was promoted by God. He lived for 140 years on earth after the experience.

Chapter 3

Are you experiencing storm?

There is a lesson that we must learn from the last chapter, we need to be weary of who we listen to when we are amid a storm. It's not strange to recall that the faith in God can get reduced, you hear words like, 'God why have you forsaken me' , are you still seated on the throne , are you Alive etc. , it might not be a good experience but managing yourself effectively counts.

During this season it's advisable you consult a matured pastor, I didn't use the word 'your pastor', it's not impossible that he might be inexperienced, you cannot offer what you don't have. Storms might be in different dimensions, but the almighty will grant wisdom that is required to handle the situation.

Jesus Christ is the only one that can calm storms no matter it's dimension and it will be wise to ensure your salvation is intact.

The storms can be in the following dimension:

1) JOB loss and you are the bread winner of the family and it happened suddenly.
2) Loss of all family members in an auto crash
3) Robbery attack on your business premises
4) Indicted in a fraud case
5) Demolition of your house
6) Huge financial loss in a transaction
7) Severe Financial crises
8) Continual loss in your business
9) Pain of strange behaviour in your only child
10) Inability to give birth
11) Death of a loved one

The list is in exhaustible but let us deal with the ones listed above and try to discuss these challenges and broker a solution to the glory of God. Before we proceed, it's pertinent to note that Mathew 11:28 -29, Jesus is ready to bear our burdens, this scripture says 'Come unto me, ye that labour and heavy laden and I will give you rest' and verse 29 says Take my yoke upon you, and learn of me; for I am meek and lowly in heart: and ye shall find rest unto your souls'

No matter how heavy your burden is, the burden bearer is ready to carry all your burdens, no matter what the issue is, it will be taken care of and I pray we key into this scripture. Apart from been a burden bearer, Jesus calms down storms, no matter the dimension , Mark 4:39 , 'And he arose, and rebuked the wind, and said unto the sea, Peace, be still. And the ceased, and there was a great calm', Jesus gives peace in the time of turbulence and instability.

One of the questions is whether you have accepted Jesus as lord as personal saviour, it might just be that he needs to get your attention for those of us facing challenges….

There is no issue that cannot be resolved with Jesus , we need him to occupy a place in our lives and there will be a great difference , Simon peter and his friends in the book of Luke 5:1-6, had given up hope as they could not catch a single fish , how will you describe this, some might call it unfruitfulness, it might as well be regarded as undesirable results which is what we call a storm.

There was an improvement when they allowed Jesus into their lives, 'Launch out into the deep, and let down your nets for a draught' and the young man told the master that they had toiled all day , but at your word we will proceed and the bible recorded that they caught all manner of fishes and their net broke and they could not carry them , they beckoned on their colleague to help them.

You can claim it but in actual sense have you allowed Jesus into your lives, please ponder on this and examine yourself , there is bound to be an improvement. Do you know whom you are, as a child of God and what you carry? , Rom 8:37 says nay in all these things we are more than conquerors through him that loved us , the storms cannot consume you because you are more than conquerors , victory is in sight.

There are times when contrary powers are responsible for our storms, these powers will bow in the name of Jesus. Why must you be afraid, psalm 62:11 , God has spoken once; twice have I heard this; that power belongeth unto God, no power supersedes the power of God and this should give us comfort and also 2 timothy 1:7 , 'For God hath not given us the spirit fear; but of power, and love, and of sound mind'

Every contrary power in operation must bow in the name of Jesus and I want us to believe that no power from the pit of hell can affect us in the name of Jesus, dispel any kind of fear , remain focused on Jesus the author and the finisher of our faith.

We must recall that faith without work is dead , as long as we are exercising faith we must ensure we put in more efforts to improve on our expertise , research into new technologies , some storms are as a result of not seeking improvement in operations etc.

A business that is bewildered with crises as a result of Errors experienced during execution of a contract , do you realize that you can pick up an insurance policy to insure all contracts annually , you are estimate your exposure per annum and when issues arises , losses can be recovered as you insurer will pay based on sum insured , this will ensure you are not thrown off balance.

We are in a country where insecurity is on the rise, we must be vigilant, security is everyone's responsibility and ensure we take precautions with respect to our business premises and adopt technologies that will improve our security , power failure could throw our premises into darkness , installing a solar powered perimeter lights can bridge this gap.

I want to encourage all our entrepreneurs to seek improvements in their businesses adopting technologies. As children of God in business we need to obey the law of the land, pay your taxes, obey laid down regulations guiding running of businesses in your locality and avoid cutting corners, this could put us in a difficult position.

Lets look at our personal life's, we have delved on business, 'Severe financial crises', we need to manage our finances and eliminate waste of resources, we need to plan. Many of us that have left paid employment must understand that there is no free money anymore, adopting the

Chinese model, 'producing what people need' and this will improve our income base, with God been on our side.

Do we recall this musician , Jide Obi , he was a successful musician in the early 80's , apparently he got born again and he sold all his property and he followed JESUS, this calls for lots of sacrifice and commitment, there is no need to mention the ministry , after a couple of months he started complaining of difficulties and blamed himself and nearly committed suicide. I'm trying to find out where he's today and what eventually happened to him after this experience.

The one that has lost loved one , you must understand that death is a debt that everyone will have to pay someday, the pain is so much when such happens and the challenge is that it can happen to anyone , young and old , there is no limit in age. We mentioned someone that lost his entire family in an accident , it requires the grace of God to counsel such a person , where will he start from with such a mishap and you might hear different kind of lamentations.

Faith in God dwindles in such individual and might want to take his own life too , road to recovery emotionally might take a long time and the counsellor has to take it easy and be patient , ensure someone is assigned to stay with the this fellow and the process of counselling continues until success is achieved. Inability to give birth , this lead to pressure from families and the couples have to unite and resist pressure from different quarters, it's not impossible that medical examination could favour these couples and this could be as a result of anxiety on the part of the wife and the Lord can do it soon.

There is no need for any frustration, but what if there is a medical complication from either of the couples , as mentioned earlier on they must be united and divorce is not an option , adopting a child from the motherless baby home will be an option. There is nothing God cannot accomplish as the turnaround is very possible, your case cannot be a difficult one for the almighty and we must remain positive and continue to trust in God. I have seen a case of barrenness for 20 years that was resolved, and your case cannot be an exception.

No matter what the challenge might be , let's trust God as the only authentic source for a resolution and we should stop depending on man , the psalmist in psalm 31:1 , 'In thee, O Lord, do I put my trust; let me never be ashamed: deliver me in thy righteousness.' , this scripture is a commitment made between man and the almighty , putting absolute trust in God and telling the almighty that he/she will not be put to shame and also psalm 33:21 ,'For our heart shall rejoice in him, because we have trusted in his holy name.' , rejoicing will be the portion for those that trust in the Lord , when there is an issue it becomes difficult to trust God , because there is no faith in God.

We should not forget the place of prayer and thanksgiving , for those facing challenges , key into psalm 50:10 -15 , before I proceed you should know whom you are , John 1:12 , 'but as many as received him, to them gave he power to become the **sons of God**, even to them that believed on his name:' , you are son and daughters of God because of your salvation experience and your remaining on track.

Don't forget Romans 8:17 , we are joint heirs of God & joint heirs with Christ and why should we be enveloped with fear if truly we are the sons/daughters of God & joint heirs , we should make efforts to visualize the personality of our father , according to the psalmist that we ought to key into , he's the richest in the entire universe , the beast of the forest and cattle upon a thousand hills belongs to him, the world is his and the fulness thereof , if he needs food he will not bother anyone, all the Lord needs from you is thanksgiving and we need to check ourselves, are we really thanking God enough or are we really living a life of gratitude to our creator,

Most of us in these challenges are not thanking God and we must improve , because with the seed of thanksgiving there are possibilities of answered prayers and look at what the lord said in verse 15 of psalm 50, 'And call upon me in the day of trouble: **I will deliver thee**, and thou shall glorify me.' , can you see with thanksgiving you have a blank cheque from the Lord in the day of adversity , he will answer and the issues will be resolved.

Don't wait till there is a challenge before we praise God, always let us cultivate the habit of praising God, because it's expected of us to do this , psalm 22:3 , 'But thou art holy, o thou that inhabitest the praises of Israel.' , Lets cultivate the habit and our lives will never remain the same.

What are the lessons about JOB, they are as follows:

1) No man on earth suffered like him
2) He remained steadfast with the Lord, despite the attacks
3) He never gave up
4) He never cursed God

5) He depended on God
6) He passed the exam set for him by Satan
7) The Lord restored him on all sides
8) He remained the richest man in the east after the restoration
9) He lived long after the experience, 140 years.

Brethren God will restore all you have lost in the name of Jesus, please don't give up.

About the Author

Alex Ndukwe, Senior Pastor at One-Accord Gospel Church , Abuja , FCT. Married to Sis Ada Ndukwe and blessed with 3 children. Deborah, David & Daniel.

www.ingramcontent.com/pod-product-compliance
Lightning Source LLC
Chambersburg PA
CBHW032103040426
42449CB00007B/1166